Contents

Eggstraspecials	8
Soupercookery	10
Finger Food	12
Special Sandwiches	14
Super Salads	16
Choose-a-Pizza	18
Hot Pots of Goodness	20
Baked Potatoes	23
Burgers	24
Meals on a Stick	26
Super Sausages	28
Viva Pasta	30
Pastry Makes	32
Fun Flans	34
Scones and Shortbread	35
Milk Shakes	38
Cakes to Bake	40
Cookies	43
Just Desserts	44
Index	46

We would like to thank the following for their help in supplying recipes and photographs used in this book:

The Butter Information Council
The Cheese Bureau
Colman Foods
The Dairy Produce Advisory Service of the Milk Marketing Board
Danish Food Centre, London
Eggs Information Bureau
Gale's Honey Bureau
Heinz Foods
Jif Lemon Bureau
The Meat Promotion Executive
New Zealand Lamb Information Bureau
Pasta Information Centre
Photo Library International
Potato Marketing Board
Spectrum Colour Library
The Sugar Bureau
Van Den Berghs
Wall's Ice Cream

Equipment used in jacket photograph kindly lent by The Reject Shop.

Copyright © MCMLXXXIV by World International Publishing Limited.
All rights reserved throughout the world.
Published in Great Britain by
World International Publishing Limited
P.O. Box 111, Great Ducie Street, Manchester M60 3BL.
Printed in Belgium.
SBN 7235 7058 2.

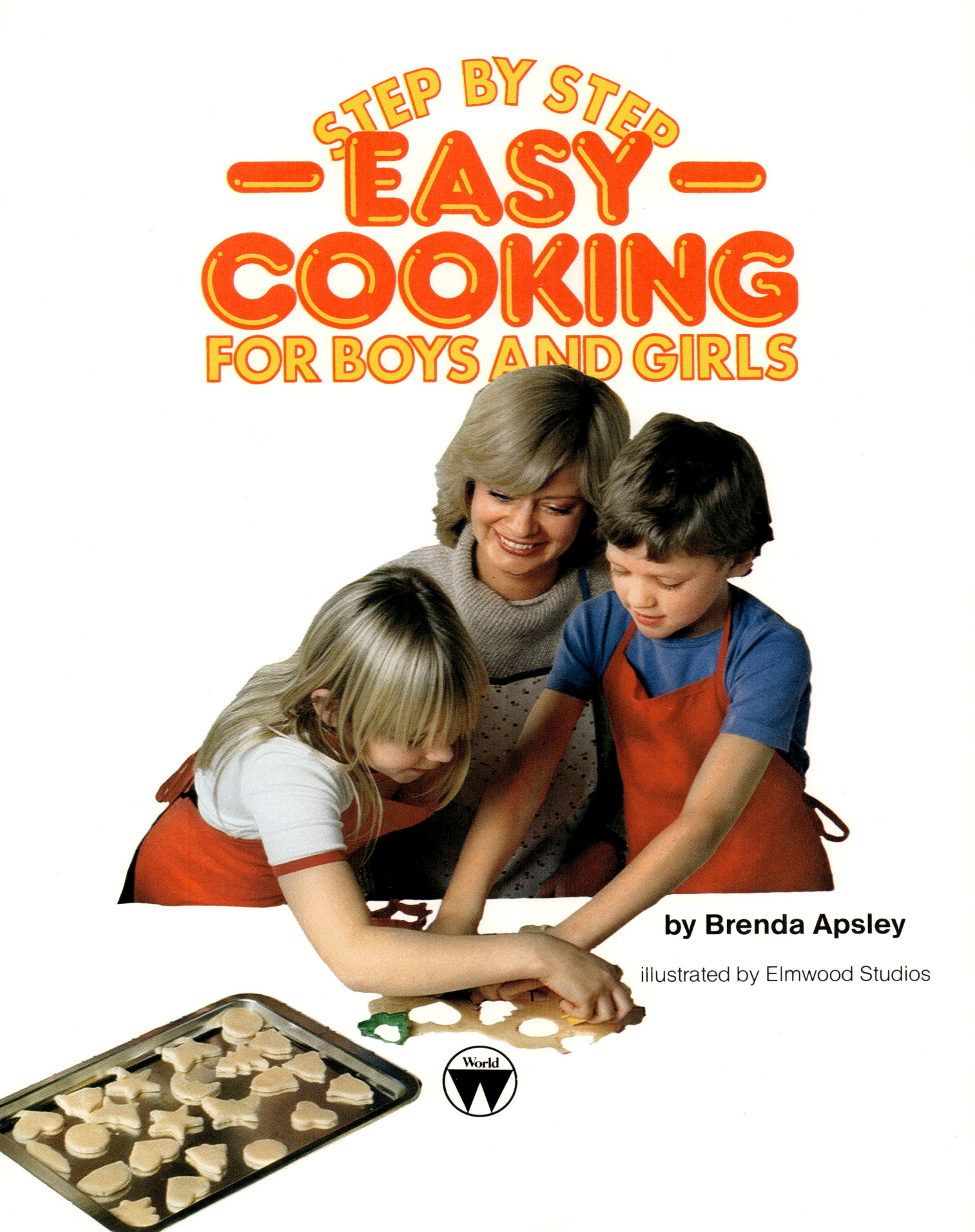

STEP BY STEP EASY COOKING FOR BOYS AND GIRLS

by Brenda Apsley

illustrated by Elmwood Studios

World

Cooking is fun, and in this book the words and pictures show you just what to do... and how to do it. But before you begin there are some important things to remember...

Safety

Always have an adult, or an older brother or sister on hand to help you, especially when lighting gas cookers.

Always use knives very carefully.

Always use oven gloves when you handle hot pans or dishes, especially when taking things from the oven.

If you have to use an eye-level grill and you can't reach it, don't stand on chairs – get help from an adult.

Turn handles on pans inwards so that they don't get knocked over.

Never touch anything electrical with wet hands – you could get a shock. If you must handle electrical appliances – like a kettle – make sure that your hands are thoroughly dry.

Hygiene

Always make sure that your hands are very clean before you begin.

Make sure that utensils and work surfaces are clean too.

Protect your clothes when you cook – wipe-clean aprons are ideal.

Remember to wash up when you've finished, and leave the kitchen clean and tidy.

Before You Begin

Read through the recipe carefully so that you know exactly what you are going to do.

Make sure that you have all the ingredients you need.

Collect all the ingredients and equipment before you begin.

Always preheat the oven. It needs time to reach the correct temperature – allow about 15 minutes before you want to use it.

Measurements

Measure liquids and solids carefully and accurately, using kitchen scales and measuring jugs.

Use metric **OR** imperial measurements – don't mix them.

All spoon measures are level spoonsful unless otherwise stated. For accuracy, skim off excess with a knife.

Presentation

Make the finished dishes look as appetising as you can. Add garnishes for colour.

If you are serving a hot dish, remember to warm plates or dishes beforehand. Put them in a cool oven for a few minutes, or plunge them into quite hot water, then dry them carefully.

U.S. Measures

Liquid:
⅓ pint (250ml) = 1 cup
Solids:
8oz (200g) = 1 cup

EGGSTRASPECIALS

Eggs are very good to eat, and you can use them in lots of different dishes. Here are some to try:

Scrambled Eggs
(serves 1)

2 eggs
2 tablespoons milk
a pinch of salt
1 tablespoon margarine

1.
In a small bowl, beat the eggs into the milk with a fork or whisk. Add a pinch of salt.

2.
Over a medium heat, melt the margarine in a small frying pan or saucepan.

3.
Pour in the egg mixture and, using a wooden spoon or spatula, stir continuously, gently pushing the mixture around the pan. It should be set, but still moist – don't overcook the eggs so that they are dry and rubbery.

4.
Serve at once on hot buttered toast.

Eggstra Scrambles

Try adding colour and flavour to basic scrambled eggs like this:

1.
Snip some parsley or fresh chives into the eggs before cooking. Serve with tomato quarters.

2.
Cut cooked ham or salami into tiny cubes and sprinkle over cooked eggs.

3.
Put a slice of cheese on top of a piece of toast and grill until it melts. Pile scrambled egg on top.

4.
Make Celery Scramble, (pictured right) for 4 people. Warm a small tin of condensed celery soup (not diluted) in a pan, add 8 beaten eggs and a pinch of salt. Cook as before.

5.
Cooled scrambled eggs make good sandwich fillers. Add a layer of fruity chutney or pickle.

Eggs Information Bureau

Home Style Beans and Eggs (serves 4)

2 tablespoons cooking oil
4oz (100g) onion
1lb (450g) potatoes
2 x 8oz (225g) tins of curried beans with sultanas
a pinch of salt
4 eggs
2oz (50g) Cheddar cheese

1.
Preheat the oven to 200°C/400°F/Gas 6.

2.
Peel the potatoes and boil in salted water until cooked – about 15 minutes. Cut into small cubes. To save time, use leftover boiled potatoes if you have them.

3.
Peel and cut the onion into thin slices.

4.
Heat the oil in a flameproof casserole dish and fry the onion for about 10 minutes until it is cooked and transparent.

5.
Stir the curried beans, diced potato and a pinch of salt into the casserole.

6.
Make four 'nests' in the potato and bean mixture with the back of a large spoon and crack an egg into each, being careful not to break the yolk.

7.
Grate the cheese and sprinkle it over the casserole. Bake for 15–20 minutes until golden, and serve with crusty bread.

Eggs Information Bureau

Egg-Bean Nests
(serves 4)

4oz (100g) streaky bacon
1 x 16oz (450g) tin baked beans
4 eggs
4 slices bread

1.
Fry the bacon until crisp and heat the beans, mix, and pour into an ovenproof dish.

2.
With a spoon, make four 'nests' in the beans, and break an egg into each.

3.
Cover with a lid and cook very gently for about 5 minutes, until the eggs are set.

4.
Toast the bread, cut into triangles, and serve as shown.

DO YOU KNOW how to tell if an egg is fresh? A fresh egg will sink in water; an old egg will float.

SOUPERCOOKERY!

Soups are tasty and warming, perfect for winter days.

Quick Potato Soup
(serves 4)

1 lb (450g) potatoes
1 large onion
2oz (50g) butter
1¾ pints (1 litre) stock
¼ pint (150ml) milk
salt and pepper
2oz (50g) Cheddar cheese
parsley

1.
Peel the potatoes and grate them on a coarse grater. Peel and grate the onion, too.

2.
Put the grated potatoes and onion in a pan with the butter, stock (made with stock cubes), and a little salt and pepper.

3.
Bring to the boil, then turn the heat low and let the soup simmer very gently for about 20 minutes, until the vegetables are soft.

4.
Add the cold milk to the soup and re-heat gently over a low heat.

5.
Pour into serving bowls, grate the Cheddar cheese and sprinkle a little on top of each serving. Sprinkle on a little chopped parsley, too.

Crusty French bread goes well with this soup. Serve it cut into chunky pieces, or hot and buttery. To do this, make cuts in a long French loaf about 1" (3cm) apart, but don't cut right through. Spread butter in the cuts, and wrap the whole loaf in kitchen foil. Put the loaf in a hot oven (220°C/425°F/Gas 7) for about 15 minutes, unwrap, and serve piping hot.

Potato Marketing Board

This soup is warming, tasty and very French!

French Onion Soup
(serves 4)

1½oz (40g) butter
1lb (450g) onions
1oz (25g) flour
2½ pints (1.5 litres) hot beef stock (made with two stock cubes)
salt and pepper
4oz (100g) cheese, Gruyere or Cheddar
a French stick loaf

1.
Peel, slice and chop the onions finely.

2.
Melt the butter in a large pan and fry the onions over a low heat for about 15 minutes until they are pale golden. Be careful not to burn them.

3.
Sprinkle on the flour and cook gently, stirring all the time with a wooden spoon, for about 4 minutes.

4.
Pour in the meat stock (made with beef stock cubes diluted in boiling water), season with salt and pepper, and simmer gently over a low heat for 20 minutes. Stir the soup from time to time.

5.
When the soup is nearly ready, slice the French loaf into thick slices and toast them on both sides.

6.
Grate the cheese and sprinkle on the toasted bread slices. Put the bread under the grill until the cheese melts.

7.
Pour the soup into warmed bowls and float bread 'rafts' on top.

Does peeling and chopping onions make you cry? Try peeling onions under running cold water, and wiping your knife with lemon juice before you begin. The most effective aid is a scuba-diving mask – if you wear one the onions won't affect you at all!

FINGER FOOD

Some food tastes better when you eat it with your fingers, doesn't it? Here are two simple dishes where fingers are best!

Barbecued Chicken Drumsticks
(serves 4)

8 small chicken drumsticks
1oz (25g) butter
1 tablespoon cooking oil
salt and pepper

sauce:

2oz (50g) butter
1 teaspoon made mustard
½ teaspoon paprika
salt
a pinch of cayenne pepper
1 teaspoon vinegar

When serving finger food, provide a fingerbowl and napkins to clean hands. Just float a couple of slices of lemon in small bowls of hot water, so that sticky fingers can be cleaned at the table.

1.
Melt 1oz (25g) butter and 1 tablespoon oil in a large frying pan over a gentle heat. Season the chicken drumsticks with salt and pepper, and fry for 10-15 minutes until golden.

2.
Test to see if the chicken is cooked through. To do this, push a thin skewer into the fattest part of a drumstick; if the juices are clear the chicken is cooked. If the juices are still pink, cook for a few minutes more and test again.

3.
For the sauce, mix the butter and mustard in a bowl using a wooden spoon, then stir in the paprika, salt, cayenne pepper and vinegar.

4.
Preheat the grill.

5.
Using a pastry brush, brush the barbecue sauce all over the cooked chicken drumsticks, and grill until hot and golden, turning so that all sides are cooked evenly.

6.
Serve just as they are!

Barbecued Lamb Riblets (serves 4)

1½lbs (¾ kilo) New Zealand breast of lamb riblets
 – ask the butcher to chop and cut these for you
2 tablespoons vinegar

sauce:

2 tablespoons soy sauce
2 tablespoons clear honey
2 tablespoons plum jam
1 tablespoon white vinegar
1 tablespoon Worcestershire sauce
1 teaspoon dry mustard powder
2 tablespoons tomato ketchup
a squeeze of lemon juice

1.
Preheat the oven to 180°C/350°F/Gas 4.

2.
Half fill a large saucepan with water, add 2 tablespoons of vinegar, and bring to the boil.

New Zealand Lamb Information Bureau

3.
Simmer the lamb riblets in the vinegar water for about 10 minutes. The lamb riblets should be separate oblong pieces; the butcher will cut them for you, or ask a parent to help.

4.
When cooked, drain the riblets on crumpled kitchen paper.

5.
Line a roasting tin with kitchen foil and lay the riblets in it, side by side.

6.
In a mixing bowl, mix all the sauce ingredients together and pour over the riblets.

7.
Bake for 30 minutes, turning the riblets once.

8.
Increase the heat to 200°C/400°F/Gas 6, and cook for another 20 minutes, turning once. The riblets should be browned, glossy and crisp.

*Serve the lamb riblets just as they are, to eat with fingers, or on a bed of buttered noodles. Use the sauce for pork ribs, too!

Special Sandwiches

The Danes know about sandwiches. They eat special open sandwiches with tasty toppings and call them *Danwiches*. Why not try some? They're fun to make — and even more fun to eat!

For an Egg and Bacon Danwich you need:

slice of bread
butter
1 hard-boiled egg, cooled
lettuce leaf, washed and dried
tomato slice
cucumber slices
mayonnaise
1 rasher streaky bacon, fried till crisp, then cooled

1.
Spread a slice of bread with butter. Cut in half.

2.
Lay a lettuce leaf on the bread. Add slices of egg so that they overlap.

3.
Spoon on some mayonnaise.

4.
Add a rasher of fried bacon.

5.
Now add the garnish. Put a slice of tomato between two slices of cucumber. Make a short slit from centre to edge, and twist.

Danish Food Centre, London

Here are some more Danwich ideas to try — or you could make up your own combinations. Remember, add different textures and different colours.

1. Fish Salad

On buttered bread add lettuce, tomato wedges, cress, one sardine and a twist of lemon.

2. Cottage Cheese Topper

Top a slice of buttered bread with a lettuce leaf, about 2oz (50g) cottage cheese, a cucumber and tomato twist, and some parsley.

3. Chef's Temptation

Top a slice of buttered bread with a lettuce leaf, a slice of cooked ham, 1 tbsp cottage cheese, ¼ pineapple ring, a gláce cherry and some parsley.

4. Chicken 'n' Cress

On a slice of buttered bread (try rye) put some watercress and a piece of cooked chicken breast. Top with an orange twist.

5. Blue Danwich

Add a lettuce leaf, a slice of Danish Blue cheese, a wedge of tomato and a stoned black grape to buttered bread.

6. Spring Salad

Top a slice of buttered rye bread with slices of cold cooked new potato, cress and a sliced radish.

SUPER SALADS

Most people think of salads as lettuce, tomato and cucumber. But salads can be very different – and they're easy to make.

Instead of mayonnaise on salads, try making French Dressing. Just put 4 tablespoons salad oil, 2 tablespoons vinegar, ½ teaspoon dry mustard powder, ½ teaspoon salt, ½ teaspoon sugar and a little black pepper into a screw-top jar and shake well. Toss salads in the dressing just before serving.

Toadstool Salad (serves 4)

4 eggs
2 large tomatoes
lettuce leaves
¼ cucumber
2 tablespoons mayonnaise

1.
Boil the eggs for about ten minutes, then plunge into cold water to cool them.

2.
When the eggs are cool, shell them, and cut a small slice from each end, so that they will stand up.

3.
Cut the tomatoes in half across the centre.

4.
Shred the lettuce finely with a knife and put on a serving plate.

5.
Peel the cucumber, slice into thin slices, and arrange on the bed of lettuce.

6.
Chop the egg ends and sprinkle them over the lettuce bed.

7.
Stand the eggs on the green salad and balance the tomato halves on top.

8.
Dot mayonnaise on the tomato halves so that they look like the marks on toadstools. Mayonnaise that comes in a tube is easy to dot on, or you could use cheese spread in a tube instead.

The only cooking here is boiling the potatoes, or you can use leftover ones.

Rosy Salad (serves 4)

1 lb (450g) potatoes
8 oz (200g) cooked ham or luncheon meat
2 eating apples
1 stick celery
1 oz (25g) seedless raisins
1 teaspoon chives
2 tablespoons mayonnaise
pinch of curry powder
lettuce leaves

1.
Peel the potatoes, quarter, and boil until tender, about 15 minutes. Drain and cool, and cut into small cubes or dice.

2.
Cut the ham or luncheon meat into small cubes.

3.
Core (but don't peel) the apples and cut them into small dice.

4.
Cut the celery into thin slices.

5.
Mix the potato, meat, apple and celery in a large bowl.

6.
Chop the chives and add them to the bowl, with the raisins, mayonnaise and curry powder.

7.
Mix all the ingredients well and leave the salad to stand for an hour.

8.
Wash and dry some lettuce leaves and use them to line a large salad bowl.

9.
Pile the potato mixture in the middle and serve.

How to core apples: Wash the apple, wipe, and cut into quarters. Remove the core and pips from each quarter and chop or slice as required. Or use a special apple corer.

Potato Marketing Board

Pizzas in Italy are usually at least as big as dinner plates; these are smaller, but still fun to make, with four different fillings to choose from.

Pizza Base (for 4 small pizzas)

8oz (200g) self-raising flour
1 teaspoon salt
1oz (25g) margarine
¼ pint (150ml) milk

1.
Preheat the oven at 230°C/450°F/Gas 8.

2.
Sieve the flour and salt into a bowl.

3.
Cut the margarine into cubes and rub lightly into the flour, using your fingertips, until the mixture looks like breadcrumbs.

4.
Add the milk and mix in with a round-blade knife, then gather the dough together lightly.

5.
Knead very lightly on a floured work surface and divide into four.

6.
With a lightly floured rolling pin, roll out each piece of dough into a 6" (15cm) circle and place them on a baking sheet.

Colman Foods

Pizza

Instead of individual pizzas, make a jumbo pizza like this one, using just the tomato layer plus cheese topping.

Tomato Layer

2 x 15oz (425g) tins of plum tomatoes
1 onion
1 teaspoon oregano
1 teaspoon basil
salt and pepper
1 teaspoon sugar
4 teaspoons mild burger mustard

1.
Drain the tomatoes, and chop them finely.

2.
Peel the onion and chop it very finely.

3.
Simmer the onions and tomatoes in a pan with the oregano, basil, salt, pepper and sugar for about 10 minutes until well blended.

4.
Spread each pizza base with a teaspoon of mild mustard.

5.
Divide the tomato mixture between the four pizza bases, spreading close to the edge.

Fillings

1. 3oz (75g) cooked ham, diced
   3oz (75g) sliced mushrooms
2. 4 slices salami
3. 4oz (100g) frozen stir-fry vegetables
4. 4 tinned sardines

Cheese Topping

8oz (200g) Cheddar or Mozzarella cheese
a little olive oil

1.
Arrange one of the fillings on each pizza base.

2.
Grate the cheese and sprinkle 2oz (50g) over each pizza.

3.
Brush lightly with olive oil and bake for 15 minutes.

When cooked the pizzas should look golden, melted, and they should smell great! Serve them just as they are, or with a green salad.

Hot pots and casseroles are easy to make. The first recipe is a simple version of the Mexican dish, chilli con carne (beans and meat) made using store-cupboard ingredients

HOT POTS

Extra Quick Chilli Con Carne (serves 4)

2 teaspoons cooking oil
1 onion
2 teaspoons chilli powder
1 x 15oz (425g) tin of minced beef in gravy
1 x 15oz (425g) tin of red kidney beans

1.
Peel and chop the onion finely.

2.
Heat the cooking oil in a medium-sized saucepan and fry the onion gently for about 10 minutes. It should be softened, but not browned.

3.
Stir in the chilli powder and cook gently for 5 minutes.

4.
Drain the liquid from the tin of beans and add them to the pan, then stir in the tin of minced beef.

5.
Heat gently until piping hot.

Serve the chilli con carne in individual dishes, with crusty rolls or slices of French loaf, or for a more filling meal, serve on a bed of boiled rice with a green salad.

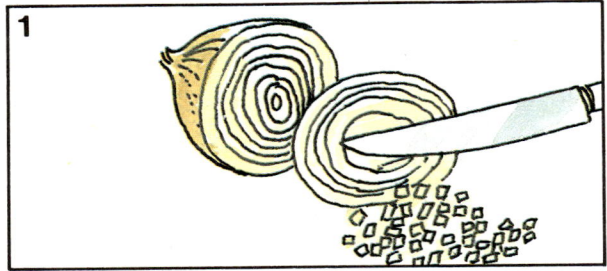

OF GOODNESS

This recipe proves that vegetables aren't boring!

Special Vegetable Layer (serves 4)

1lb (450g) potatoes
½ cauliflower
8oz (200g) carrots
2oz (50g) mushrooms
4oz (100g) green beans, tinned or frozen
4oz (100g) Cheddar cheese
2 eggs
½ pint (250ml) milk
salt and pepper

1.
Preheat the oven at 180°C/350°F/Gas 4.

2. Peel the potatoes and slice them into rings about ¼" (5mm) wide.

3.
Wash the cauliflower and break it into small 'florets'.

4.
Wash, peel and slice the carrots into rings.

5.
Wash the mushrooms and slice finely.

6.
Grate the Cheddar cheese.

7.
Put layers of potato, cauliflower, carrot, mushroom, green beans and grated cheese into a buttered casserole dish. Repeat until all the vegetables are used up, finishing with a layer of cheese.

8.
Beat the eggs, milk, salt and pepper and pour over the vegetables.

9.
Cook for 1½ hours in the oven until set and golden brown.

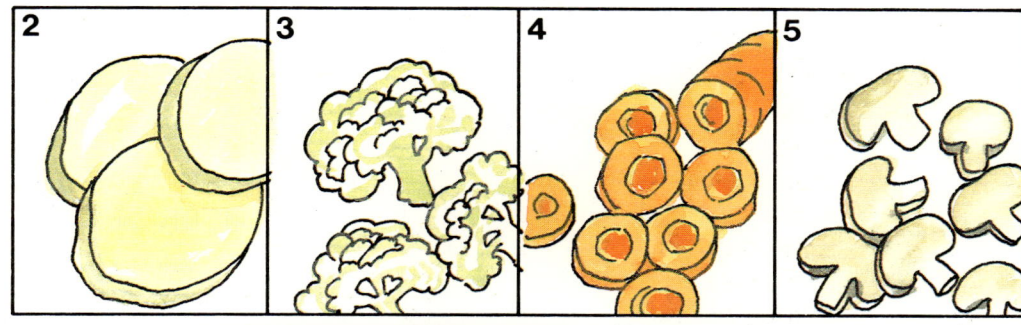

Serve with crusty white bread or wholemeal rolls.

The Dairy Produce Advisory Service of the Milk Marketing Board

A REAL WINTER WARMER

Winter Pork and Bean Hotpot (serves 4)

2 tablespoons cooking oil
4oz (100g) onion
1lb (450g) pork shoulder
8oz (225g) carrots
½ chicken stock cube
¼ pint (150ml) water
2 x 8oz (225g) tins of curried beans with sultanas
a dash of Worcestershire sauce
salt
parsley

1.
Peel and chop the onion finely, and fry in cooking oil in a medium saucepan until transparent, about 10 mins over a gentle heat.

2.
Cube the pork if your butcher hasn't already done so, and brown on all sides in the pan. This should take about 10 minutes.

3.
Peel and chop the carrots into thick slices, and add to the pan.

4.
Add the half stock cube and water, bring to the boil, then cover with a well-fitting lid and simmer gently over a low heat for 1 hour.

5.
Stir in the tins of curried beans with sultanas.

6.
Add a dash of Worcestershire sauce and a little salt.

7.
Heat the casserole through on a low heat until piping hot, and sprinkle with a little fresh chopped parsley if you have any.

Serve just as it is, or with crusty French bread slices or pitta breads (from supermarkets).

Baked Potatoes

For each person, take one large, even potato (about 8oz/ 250g) and scrub it clean, removing any 'eyes'.

Prick all over with a fork and bake in a pre-heated oven at 200°C/400°F/Gas 6 for about 1 hour, depending on size. Test to see if they are cooked by pushing in a fork.

Cut a cross in each potato and serve with butter, salt and pepper.

Stuffed Baked Potatoes

To make stuffed baked potatoes, bake the potatoes as above, but instead of a cross, cut a 'lid' from the top of each one. Scoop out some of the cooked potato, mix with the filling, and pile back into the shell. Re-heat in the oven for about 10 minutes.

Try these fillings, or invent your own! Amounts are for each potato.

2 tablespoons baked beans

2 tablespoons coleslaw

1 large chopped Frankfurter sausage

2oz (50g) grated cheese

2 tinned sardines, mashed

1oz (25g) cream cheese and a little finely chopped onion

Birds in the Nest

For this tasty dish, bake the potatoes as before, take off 'lids' and scoop out some of the cooked potato. Mix it with a little butter, salt and pepper, pile back into the shell and press down well, making a hole or 'nest'. Carefully, break an egg into each potato nest and put the potatoes back in the oven for about 10 minutes, until the egg is cooked and set.

BURG

If you've never eaten a real home-made burger, now's the time to try one!

Basic Burgers (makes 6)

1 lb (450g) lean minced beef
1 egg
salt and pepper

1.
Beat the egg lightly.

2.
In a bowl, mix the beef, beaten egg, salt and pepper with your fingers.

3.
Divide the mixture into six and roll into balls.

4.
On a floured board or worktop, flatten the balls into 4" (10cm) rounds.

5.
Heat a little oil in a frying pan.

6.
Fry the burgers for 5–8 minutes on one side, then turn over and repeat until cooked through. Or grill, if you prefer.

*Extras

Add extra flavour to the basic burger mix by adding 1 small onion, finely chopped, to the raw meat, or two pinches of dried mixed herbs.

Barbecue Burgers

Add a tasty sauce to the basic burger.

In a small pan heat:
gently until the sugar has dissolved.

Use hot or cold.

1 tablespoon tomato ketchup
½ tablespoon made mild mustard
2 tablespoons vinegar
2 tablespoons brown sugar

Serve your burgers American-style, on split, toasted buns with one – or some – or all! – of the following:

lettuce
raw onion rings
tomato ketchup
mayonnaise
mustard
coleslaw
cheese slices
sweet pickle
crispy fried bacon
pickled gherkin slices

Here's a burger-with-a-difference. If you like sausages, you'll love . . .

Sausage Burgers
(makes 4)

½lb (200g) sausage meat, pork or beef
1 medium onion
1oz (25g) butter
2 heaped tablespoons fresh white breadcrumbs
1 cooking apple
salt and pepper
1 egg

1.
Peel and chop the onion finely, and fry in butter till soft – about 5–8 minutes.

2.
Peel, core and grate the cooking apple.

3.
In a bowl, mix the sausage meat, breadcrumbs, grated apple, cooked onion, salt and pepper.

4.
Beat the egg lightly and add to the mixture to bind it together.

5.
Divide the mixture into four and, on a floured work surface, shape the mixture into four flat rounds.

6.
Fry the burgers in a greased frying pan over a gentle heat for about 10 minutes each side.

Serve the Sausage Burgers piping hot on split toasted muffins or sesame seed rolls. If you like them, add fried onion rings.

Spectrum Colour Library

Breadcrumbs

To make breadcrumbs, cut off crusts from slices and grate the bread on a coarse grater.
If there is a liquidiser or food processor in your kitchen, it will crumb small cubes of bread, but you must let an adult do this for you.

25

MEALS ON

In Turkey hundreds of years ago the Caucasus mountain people put pieces of meat (usually lamb) on their swords and cooked it over an open fire. They called the food kebabs, and now they are eaten all over the world, though they are no longer cooked on swords!

Kebabs are usually cooked over an open barbecue fire, or under a hot grill. Small cubes of meat, fish and vegetables about 1" (3cm) square are threaded onto long skewers, seasoned, and cooked for about 15 minutes. Skewers should be greased first, meat and fish should be lean, and the skewers should be turned as they cook so that the food cooks evenly.

As for ingredients – anything goes! Make your own combinations, but always vary textures and colours as well as flavours. Try these kebabs:

Lamb Kebabs

Alternate cubes of lean lamb with baby onions (or segments), tomato quarters, small mushrooms and squares of red pepper. Season with salt and pepper before cooking and for extra flavour brush on a little mint jelly or dried mint.

Ham or Gammon Kebabs

Thread your kebab skewers with alternate cubes of lean ham or gammon, pineapple chunks, small whole mushrooms, small onions or onion pieces and squares of green pepper. If you like a strong pineapple flavour, brush a little pineapple juice over the assembled kebabs, season with salt and pepper and grill.

Fish Kebabs

Try cubes of white fish fillet (cod is good) with green pepper squares, celery, onion and tomato segments and lemon wedges. Add a few black or green grapes if you have them, and for extra lemony flavour brush the kebab with a little lemon juice before cooking.

A STICK

Beef Kebabs

Alternate cubes of lean beef with courgette slices, onion segments, whole mushrooms, orange segments and one or two bay leaves. The bay leaves are only for flavour – don't eat them!

Vegetable Kebabs

If you don't eat meat, make tasty vegetable kebabs with onion and celery chunks, slices of courgette, whole mushrooms, whole baby tomatoes and chunks of apple. Add a little apple juice before cooking for extra flavour.

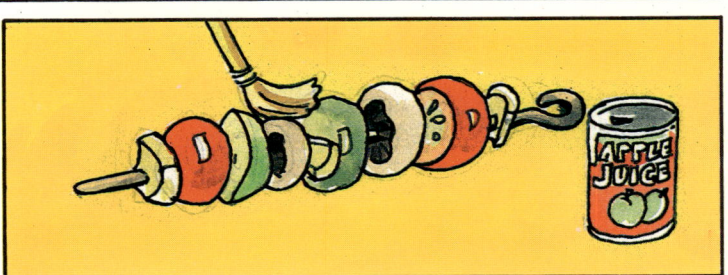

Chicken Kebabs

Take small cubes of skinned, boned, lean chicken (breast is ideal) and thread them onto skewers with baby tomatoes and onions, mushrooms and slices of frankfurter sausage. Roll up rashers of streaky bacon and thread these on, too.

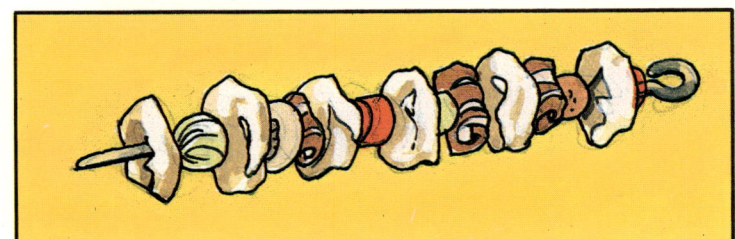

Fruit Kebabs

Different! Use chunks of apple, banana, orange and lemon segments, pineapple chunks and a few grapes, and cook for about 10 minutes. Sprinkle on a little brown sugar or brush on some honey before grilling for a special sticky glaze.

Serve kebabs on a bed of plain boiled rice cooked according to the instructions on the package, on a bed of green salad, or in split pitta breads from supermarkets and delicatessens.

Have a kebab party! Have cubed foods ready and let your friends make up their own kebabs.

Super Sausages

Sausages taste good on their own, in hot dogs, or on top of a mashed-potato mountain. They are extra good with tinned spaghetti and baked beans, too, as these two simple recipes show:

Pasta-Banger Specials (makes 4)

4 crisp bread rolls – long or round
butter
1 x 15oz (450g) tin spaghetti rings in tomato sauce
4 pork sausages

1.
Preheat the oven at 180°C/350°F/Gas 4.

2.
Cut a slice from the top of each bread roll and scoop out most of the bread to make hollow bread 'shells'. Use the breadcrumbs in stuffings etc.

3.
Spread the insides of the rolls with butter.

4.
Fry the sausages until cooked and golden, and cut into 1" (3cm) chunks.

5.
Mix the sausage chunks and spaghetti hoops and fill each bread roll.

6.
Heat through in the oven for about 20 minutes.

*If you like, add a little grated cheese to the top of each 'special' before putting them into the oven.

Pasta Information Centre

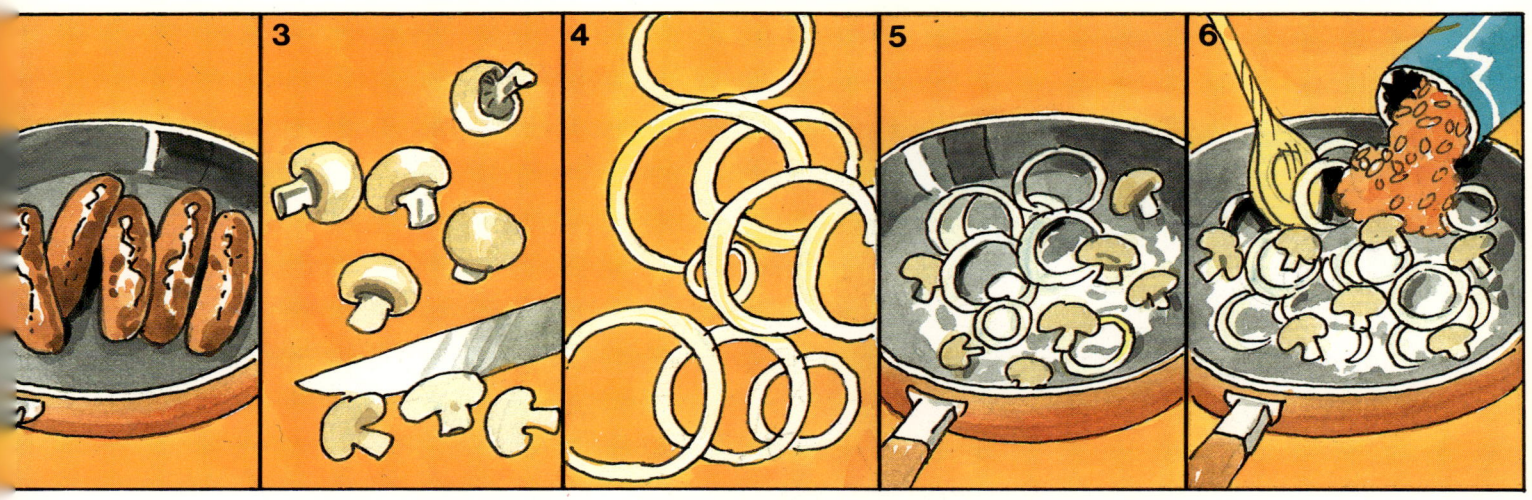

Sausage Bean Feast (serves 6)

1 lb (450g) pork sausages, thick or thin
4oz (100g) mushrooms
2 onions
1 tablespoon cooking oil
1 15oz (450g) tin of baked beans in tomato sauce
a dash of Worcestershire sauce
salt and pepper
2 tomatoes

1.
Preheat the oven at 190°C/375°F/Gas 5.

2.
Grill or fry the sausages until they are cooked and golden.

3.
Wash, dry and slice the mushrooms.

4.
Peel the onion and slice it finely.

5.
Heat the oil in a frying pan and fry the mushrooms and onions gently for about 10 minutes.

6.
Stir in the baked beans, add a dash of Worcestershire sauce, and some salt and pepper.

7.
Put the bean mixture into an ovenproof dish and arrange the cooked sausages on top.

8.
Cut the tomatoes into thin wedges and arrange them on top of the casserole.

9.
Heat in the oven for 10 minutes, and serve piping hot.

VIVA PASTA!

Pasta (Latin: a paste) was probably invented by the Chinese 6,000 years ago. It is now eaten all over the world (especially in Italy) and comes in hundreds of shapes and sizes. These recipes use two familiar kinds of pasta – macaroni and spaghetti.

Macaroni Cheese
(serves 4)

6oz (150g) short-cut macaroni
1oz (25g) butter
1oz (25g) plain flour
¾ pint (375ml) milk
1 teaspoon made mustard
salt and pepper
6oz (150g) Cheddar cheese

1.
Cook the macaroni in lots of boiling, salted water for 10 minutes. Drain and keep warm. If you use quick-cook macaroni, follow the directions on the packet.

2.
Melt the butter in a saucepan over a gentle heat, and stir in the flour with a wooden spoon to make a paste.

3.
Gradually add the milk, stirring, and bring to the boil to make a smooth sauce.

4.
Add the made mustard, salt and pepper and simmer, stirring, for 3-4 minutes.

5.
Grate the Cheddar cheese and stir 4oz (100g) into the sauce.

6.
Stir in the macaroni and put the mixture into a pie dish. Sprinkle the remaining 2oz (50g) cheese on top, and brown under a hot grill.

Serve with tomato rings and triangles of hot buttered toast.

Vary the recipe if you like! Try adding 2oz (50g) chopped cooked ham, 2oz (50g) chopped, fried onions, or 2oz (50g) fried mushroom slices.

This famous Italian dish is served in the top restaurants. Yet it's simple to make at home.

Spaghetti Bolognese
(serves 4)

Bolognese Sauce:

3 tablespoons cooking oil
1 large onion
8oz (200g) minced beef
1 tablespoon plain flour
1 small tin of plum tomatoes
½ beef stock cube
salt and pepper
½ teaspoon dried mixed herbs
½ teaspoon powdered sweet paprika
¼ pint (125ml) boiling water

1.
Heat the oil in a medium saucepan.

2.
Peel and chop the onion. Fry in the oil for about 10 minutes over a low heat.

3.
Add the minced beef. With a wooden spoon, stir and break up the mince until it is cooked, brown and crumbly. This will take about 10 minutes.

4.
Add the flour, chopped tomatoes (and their juice), half stock cube, salt and pepper, herbs and paprika, and stir well.

5.
Add the hot water, stir well, and put on a tight-fitting lid. Turn down the heat and simmer gently for 25 minutes.

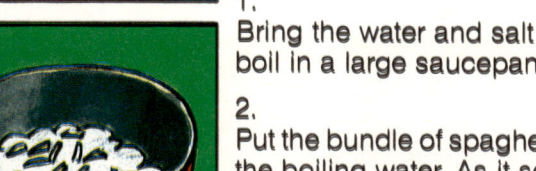

Spaghetti:
3½ pints (2 litres) water
1 teaspoon salt
8oz (200g) spaghetti
1 tablespoon olive oil

1.
Bring the water and salt to the boil in a large saucepan.

2.
Put the bundle of spaghetti into the boiling water. As it softens, bend it and push it down until it is all under the water.

3.
Add the olive oil (which stops the spaghetti strands sticking together) and stir once, then boil for 15 minutes.

4.
Drain the spaghetti in a sieve or colander, and put into a warmed serving dish.

Serve the dish like this:
Top heaps of spaghetti with the Bolognese sauce and, for a real Italian flavour, add a little grated Parmesan cheese.

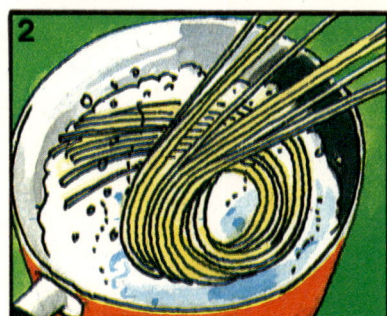

Speedy Tuna Spaghetti
is super-quick, super tasty!

1.
Cook 12oz (300g) spaghetti as above.

2.
Mix a 10oz (250g) tin of condensed mushroom soup with a 7oz (175g) tin of tuna (drained and flaked), and 2oz (50g) grated Cheddar cheese. Heat gently in a saucepan.

3.
Pile the sauce on top of the cooked, drained spaghetti and top with 1oz (25g) lightly crushed potato crisps.

Pastry

Shortcrust pastry has lots of uses in the kitchen, for both savoury and sweet dishes. It is easy to make, but there are some important points to remember:

To make 8oz (200g) Shortcrust Pastry you will need:

8oz (200g) plain flour
pinch salt
2oz (50g) margarine
2oz (50g) lard
about 2 tablespoons cold water
flour for dredging

1.
Using a sieve, sift the flour and salt into a large mixing bowl.

2.
Cut the lard and margarine into small cubes and add them to the flour and salt.

3.
Rub the fat into the flour with your fingertips, as lightly as you can, until the mixture looks like fine breadcrumbs.

4.
Sprinkle over 2 tablespoons of cold water and mix with a round-blade knife until the mixture begins to cling together. Add a few drops more if the mixture is too dry.

5.
With your hands, gather the dough together into a ball.

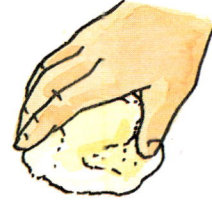

6.
On a lightly floured surface, knead the dough lightly. Do this by gently folding the dough from the outside to the centre, until it is smooth.

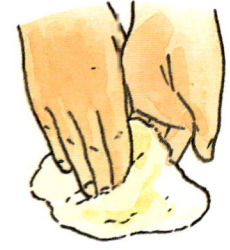

7.
If you have time, put the dough into the refrigerator to chill for about 30 minutes.

8.
When you are ready to roll out, sprinkle the work surface and rolling pin with a little flour and roll with short forward strokes, turning the dough clockwise after each rolling, so that the pastry is an even thickness. Roll out to a thickness of about 1/8" (3mm).

# makes

- Keep everything cool. Use ...ts from the refrigerator, use ...old or iced water, and wash ...ands in cold water before ...ou begin.
- ...on't add too much water.
- Handle the pastry as little as possible – treat it very gently.
- Try to allow time to chill the pastry before rolling out.
- When rolling out, use the minimum amount of flour.

Lemon Curd Tarts

8oz (200g) shortcrust pastry (see opposite page)
6-8 tablespoons lemon curd

1.
Preheat the oven at 190°C/375°F/Gas 5.

2.
Grease a 12-hole bun or tartlet tin.

3.
Make the shortcrust pastry as shown on the opposite page.

4.
Roll out to a thickness of about ⅛" (3mm) and, using a pastry cutter, cut out rings. You should get about 12.

5.
Put the pastry circles into the tin and put about a teaspoonful of lemon curd into each one.

6.
If you have any pastry left over, cut out tiny circles, or heart shapes like the ones shown here, and put them on top of the lemon curd.

7.
Bake the tarts for 10-15 minutes. The pastry should be light and golden when cooked.

8.
Leave the tarts to cool before serving. Don't be tempted to eat them straight from the oven – the lemon curd will be very hot.

Jam Tarts

You can make Jam Tarts in just the same way, using jam instead of lemon curd. Try making six of each!

Jif Lemon Bureau

Fun Flans

Flans are fun to make – and even more fun to eat.

Bean and Vegetable Flan

Pastry:

4oz (100g) plain flour
pinch salt
1oz (25g) lard
1oz (25g) margarine
1 tablespoon cold water

Filling:

4oz (100g) carrots
4oz (100g) onion
2 eggs
1oz (25g) margarine
1 x 15oz (450g) can of baked beans
½ teaspoon dried thyme
salt and pepper

1.
Preheat the oven at 190°C/375°F/Gas 5.

2.
Make the shortcrust pastry as shown on page 32 and roll it out into a circle about 10" (25cm) in diameter.

3.
Using a rolling pin to lift the pastry, line an 8" (20cm) flan ring or sandwich cake tin, trimming off any spare pastry by rolling the pin across the top.

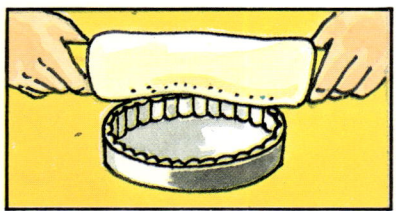

4.
Peel and dice the carrots, and peel and chop the onion into small pieces.

5.
Melt the margarine in a small pan, fry the carrots and onions gently until soft. This should take about 10 minutes over a gentle heat. Put aside to cool.

6.
Beat the eggs, stir in the baked beans and the thyme, and season with salt and pepper.

7.
Stir in the cooled carrots and onions and pour the mixture into

the pastry case. Cook in the oven for about 45 minutes, until firm.

TIP! Metal flan rings make the best pastry!

Scones and shortbread

Scones and shortbread are easy to make – and easy to eat. Make some for someone you like – or just for yourself.

Scones (makes about 12)

8oz (200g) self-raising flour
1 level teaspoon salt
2 tablespoons granulated sugar
2oz (50g) margarine (block)
¼ pint (125ml) milk

1.
Preheat the oven to 230°C/450°F/Gas 8.

2.
Sieve the salt and flour into a mixing bowl and cut the margarine into cubes.

3.
Using your fingertips, lightly rub the margarine into the flour until the mixture looks like fine breadcrumbs. Don't over rub.

4.
Stir in the sugar.

5.
With a round-blade knife, mix the milk into the flour. You should have a soft dough, moist but not too sticky.

6.
Turn the dough onto a floured board or worktop and knead it very lightly. Do this by folding the dough from the outside to the centre, turning the dough, until it is smooth and firm, with no cracks.

7.
Dust a rolling pin with a little flour and, on a floured surface, roll the dough firmly and evenly until it is ½" (12mm) thick. Do not roll the dough thinner than this.

8.
Take a pastry cutter 2" (5cm) across, dip it in flour, and cut out scone shapes. You should get about 12.

9.
Grease a baking sheet or tray (margarine wrappers are good for this) and lay the scones on it. Bake the scones in the top of the oven for about 10 minutes.

10.
The scones should be soft inside, crisp and golden outside. Cool them on a wire rack.

*Eat the scones just as they are, or split and spread with butter, or filled with thick cream and jam.

There are lots of different kinds of scones, all made in the same basic way. Here are three to try:

Spicy Scones

Sieve 2 level teaspoons ground mixed spice into the flour, add 1oz (25g) sultanas with the sugar, then make as before.

Scones don't have to be sweet. Try these special

Cheese Scones with Creamed Cheese Filling (makes 12)

8oz (200g) self-raising flour
1 level teaspoon salt
½ level teaspoon dry mustard powder
1oz (25g) butter or margarine
4oz (100g) Cheddar cheese
¼ pint (125ml) milk

filling:

4oz (100g) Cheddar cheese
salt and pepper
3 – 4 tablespoons single
   cream or top of the milk

1.
Preheat the oven to 230°C/450°F/Gas 8.

2.
Sieve the flour, salt and mustard into a bowl, and rub in the fat as before.

3.
Grate the cheese, stir into the flour, and bind together with the milk.

4.
Knead lightly, roll and cut out as before, put on a greased baking tray. Bake for 10 minutes, then leave to cool.

5.
For the filling, grate the cheese, and mix it well with the salt, pepper and cream or milk until smooth.

*Serve the scones split and filled with the creamed cheese filling. Add extra taste by adding 1 tablespoon tomato ketchup to the filling.

Fruit Scones

Make plain scones as before, but add 2oz (50g) currants with the sugar. If you like it, add a little chopped candied peel, too.

Wholemeal Scones

Instead of using all white flour, use 6oz (150g) wholemeal brown flour, and 2oz (50g) white flour. Do not add the sugar. These taste good warm for breakfast with marmalade.

The Cheese Bureau

Shortbread (makes 24 biscuits)

12oz (350g) plain flour
4oz (100g) caster sugar
8oz (200g) butter

1.
Preheat the oven at 160°C/325°F/Gas 3, and grease a baking tray.

2.
Sift the flour and salt into a bowl. Cut the butter into cubes and, using your fingertips, rub in until the mixture starts to bind together.

3.
Knead the mixture lightly (see the previous page for how to do this). Divide into three equal amounts and roll out into three circles about 7" (18cm) across.

4.
Pinch the edges between thumb and finger, mark each circle into eight with a knife, and put on the baking tray.

5.
Bake for about 20 minutes until crisp and golden, cool on the baking tray and sprinkle with a little extra caster sugar. When cool, break into triangles.

*Try Coconut Shortbread. Just sprinkle a little desiccated coconut onto the shortbread about 5 minutes before the end of cooking time.

If you prefer, roll the shortbread into rectangles, then mark into fingers.

Honey and Ginger Shortbread
(makes 24 pieces)

12oz (350g) plain flour
6oz (175g) butter
2oz (50g) caster sugar
3 rounded tablespoons set honey
4oz (100g) crystallized ginger

1.
Rub the butter into the flour and sugar as before, then mix in the honey and the ginger, finely chopped.

2.
Knead, roll into three circles, mark into portions and bake as before.

Gale's Honey Bureau

Milk Shakes

Milk drinks are tasty, nutritious, refreshing — and very easy to make. Try these recipes, which all serve one!

Lime-Lemon Shake

½ pint (250ml) chilled milk
2 tablespoons lime juice cordial
slice of lemon

1. Whisk the cordial into the milk.
2. Add a slice of lemon and straws.

Berry Milkshake

½ pint (250ml) chilled milk
1 tablespoon instant dessert mix, raspberry strawberry
1 scoop icecream

1. Whisk icecream into milk.
2. Whisk dessert mix into milk.

Hot Mocha Milk

½ pint (250ml) milk
2 teaspoons drinking chocolate
1 teaspoon instant coffee
1 tablespoon fresh cream

1. Bring the milk to the boil, take off heat and cool. Pour into a glass.
2. Add drinking chocolate and coffee and stir well.
3. Stir in fresh cream.

Chocolate Milkshake

½ pint (250ml) chilled milk
3-4 teaspoons drinking chocolate
1 tablespoon vanilla icecream
1 chocolate flake bar

1. Dissolve drinking chocolate in a little hot water, and cool.
2. Add to milk, then float icecream on top.
3. Add chocolate flake bar.

Cream Chocolate

½ pint (250ml) milk
⅛ pint (65ml) whipping cream
2oz (50g) plain chocolate
pinch of ground cinnamon

1. In a pan, heat the milk, chocolate and cinnamon until dissolved.
2. Bring to the boil.
3. Whip the fresh cream and whisk most of it into the milk.
4. Pour into glass and top with remaining fresh cream and cinnamon.

Honey-Grapefruit Shake

¼ pint (125ml) chilled milk
¼ pint (125ml) grapefruit juice
½ tablespoon clear honey

1. Mix the milk, grapefruit juice and honey until thick and frothy. An electric blender does this quickly and easily.

Banana Milkshake

½ pint (300ml) chilled milk
1 tablespoon drinking chocolate
2oz (50g) natural yogurt
½ banana, mashed
a few chopped walnuts

1. Whisk the milk, drinking chocolate, yogurt and banana until smooth.
2. Pour into a tall glass and sprinkle with chopped nuts.

Cakes to Bake

Honey Gingerbread

This is good to eat – and very quick and easy to make.

4oz (100g) butter
4oz (100g) brown sugar
4 tablespoons set honey
2 eggs
8oz (225g) plain flour
1 tablespoon ground ginger
1 level teaspoon bicarbonate of soda
1oz (25g) mixed dried fruit

1.
Preheat the oven to 180°C/350°F/Gas 4, and grease and line a 6" x 8" (15cm x 20cm) square cake tin with greaseproof paper. Ask an adult to help if you've never done this before.

2.
Beat the eggs in a small basin with a fork.

3.
In a small pan, heat the butter, sugar and honey over a low heat until they have melted.

4.
Remove the pan from the heat and mix in the beaten eggs.

5.
Mix the flour, ginger and bicarbonate of soda in a bowl and stir into the mixture in the pan. Add the fruit, too, using a wooden spoon.

6.
Put the mixture into the lined cake tin and bake for 35 minutes.

7.
When the time is up, test the cake – it should feel springy. If not, cook for another 5 minutes.

8.
Using oven gloves, take the cake from the oven, turn it onto a wire rack to cool, then serve cut into fingers.

The Sugar Bureau

Here's a cake with a difference – you don't cook it in the oven, but chill it in the fridge instead! It's very easy.

No-Bake Cake

4oz (100g) margarine
2 rounded tablespoons golden syrup
8oz (200g) digestive biscuits
2oz (50g) raisins
2 level tablespoons cocoa powder

1.
Grease a 7" (18cm) round or square cake tin.

2.
In a small pan, melt the margarine and golden syrup over a very low heat. As soon as the margarine has melted, remove from the heat.

3.
Break up the digestive biscuits into fine crumbs. An easy way to do this is to put the biscuits into a plastic bag, seal the end, and crush with a rolling pin.

4.
Put the biscuit crumbs, raisins and cocoa powder in a bowl.

5.
Stir in the melted margarine and syrup and mix everything well.

6.
Press and flatten the mixture in the cake tin and put into the refrigerator for a couple of hours until it is quite cool, then turn out and serve.

Decorate with small sweets, pieces of chocolate flake bar, chocolate buttons or hundreds and thousands. Press these into the cake while it is still soft, before you cool it in the fridge.

This cake is ultra-easy – you don't even have to weigh out the ingredients, as all the measuring is done with one cup and a teaspoon! It can't fail!

Quick Cup Cake

1 cup milk
1 cup dried mixed fruit
1 cup brown sugar
2 cups self-raising flour
1 teaspoon mixed spice

1.
Preheat the oven at 180°C/350°F/Gas 4.

2.
Grease a 1lb (450g) loaf tin.

3.
Using a good-sized tea cup, measure all the ingredients into a large mixing bowl.

4.
Mix well with a wooden spoon or spatula.

5.
Put the mixture into the loaf tin and bake for 1 hour.

6.
Serve in slices – add butter if you like.

The Dairy Produce Advisory Service of the Milk Marketing Board

cookies

Special party-time – anytime – cookies.

Biscuit Base

8oz (200g) plain flour
2oz (50g) lard
2oz (50g) margarine
pinch of salt
3oz (75g) caster sugar
1 orange
1 egg

Icing

6oz (150g) icing sugar
1–2 tablespoons orange juice
few drops of food colouring
few small coloured sweets

1.
Preheat the oven to 150°C/300°F/Gas 2 and grease a baking sheet.

2.
Sieve the flour and salt into a bowl and rub in the cubed lard and margarine (see page 32), until the mixture looks like fine breadcrumbs.

3.
Using a fine grater, grate the rind of the orange (not the white pith) and add it to the mixture with the caster sugar. Stir in.

4.
Beat the egg and add it, mixing to make a soft dough.

5.
With your hands, knead the mixture on a floured surface, folding gently, until the dough is smooth.

6.
Roll out with a rolling pin until the dough is about ⅛" (3mm) thick.

7.
Using shaped biscuit cutters, cut the dough into rounds, squares, moons, stars, triangles – anything you like – and put the cookies on the baking tray.

8.
Bake for 30 minutes, then cool on a wire tray before icing.

9.
For the icing, put the icing sugar, orange juice (squeezed from the orange) and a few drops of food colouring into a bowl.

10.
Beat with a wooden spoon until smooth and glossy.

11.
Using a teaspoon, put a little icing onto each cookie and, before the icing sets, decorate with small coloured sweets.

Van Den Berghs

43

Ice cream makes simple, quick desserts. Here are three delicious recipes to try.

Just Desserts

Beehives (serves 4)

a tub of soft scoop vanilla ice cream
4 tablespoons clear honey
2oz (50g) rice crispies

1.
Put two scoops or spoonsful of ice cream onto each serving plate.

2.
Pour 1 tablespoon of honey over each portion, and sprinkle over ½oz (12g) of rice crispies. That's it!

*Beehives taste good with brandy snaps.

Neapolitan Sail Boats (serves 4)

a block of neapolitan ice cream
2 straws
rice paper

1.
Cut 4 thick slices of ice cream and put one on each plate.

2.
Cut straws in half and press one half into each ice cream slice.

3.
Cut out triangles of rice paper and put two on each ice cream slice as sails.

*If you like, add a few colourful sweets to each serving.

Strawberry Ice Cream Shortbreads (serves 4)

4 round, bought shortbreads
8oz (200g) fresh strawberries
a tub of soft scoop strawberry ice cream

1.
Cut the strawberries in half, but leave four large ones whole.

2.
Put strawberry halves on each shortbread ring and spoon ice cream on top.

3.
Top each portion with a whole strawberry

*Shortbreads can be bought in packets from shops and supermarkets. Or you could make your own – see page 37.

44

Here's a special dessert made with yogurt.

Yogurt Mallow (serves 4)

2 egg whites
2oz (50g) caster sugar
1 small carton of yogurt, any flavour
1 tablespoon desiccated coconut

1.
First separate the egg whites. Crack each egg over a cup very carefully. Pass the yolk from one half shell to the other, letting the white run into the cup. Don't break the yolks.

2.
Whisk the egg whites using a wire balloon whisk or a rotary whisk. Use a very clean, grease-free bowl. The whites should be foamy, stiff and firm.

3.
When stiff, whisk the sugar into the egg whites.

4.
Now fold in the yogurt. Do this very carefully, using a large metal spoon. Cut and turn with the spoon, in a figure of 8 movement, carefully, until the yogurt is mixed in. Spoon into serving glasses.

5.
Now toast the coconut. Toast it under the grill, turning with a fork, until it is evenly browned. Don't let it burn.

6
Sprinkle the toasted coconut over each serving.

*For extra flavour, try adding chopped fresh or tinned fruit to the yogurt mallow. Hazelnut yogurt with chopped banana is great!

Eggs Information Bureau

Knickerbocker Glory

Here's a fun dessert to make. It looks great, and tastes even better. You need slices of strawberry, fresh cream (whipped till stiff), sliced tinned peaches, vanilla ice cream and chopped nuts. Layer them all in a tall glass and there you have it – Knickerbocker Glory!

45

Index

A
Apples, how to core   17

B
Baked Potatoes   23
Banana Milkshake   39
Barbecue Burgers   24
Barbecued Chicken Drumsticks   12
Barbecued Lamb Riblets   13
Bean and Vegetable Flan   34
Beans, Home Style with Eggs   9
Beans, Winter Pork Hotpot   22
Beef Kebabs   27
Beehives   44
Berry Milkshake   38
Birds in the Nest   23
Blue Danwich   15
Breadcrumbs   25
Burgers   24-25

C
Cakes   41-42
Celery Scramble   8
Cheese, Macaroni   30
Cheese Scones with Creamed Cheese Filling   36
Chef's Temptation Danwich   15
Chicken, Barbecued Drumsticks   12
Chicken and Cress Danwich   15
Chicken Kebabs   27
Chilli Con Carne, Extra Quick   20
Chocolate Milkshake   39
Cookies   43
Cottage Cheese Topper Danwich   15
Cream Chocolate   39

D
Danwiches   14-15

E
Eggs, Scrambled   8
Egg and Bacon Danwich   14
Egg-Bean Nests   9
Extra Quick Chilli Con Carne   20

F
Fish Kebabs   26
Fish Salad Danwich   15
French Dressing   16
French Onion Soup   11
Fruit Kebabs   27
Fruit Scones   36

G
Gammon Kebabs   26
Gingerbread, Honey   40

H
Ham Kebabs   26
Home Style Beans and Eggs   9
Honey and Ginger Shortbread   37
Honey Gingerbread   40
Honey-Grapefruit Shake   39
Hot Mocha Milk   38

I
Ice Cream Desserts   44-45

J
Jam Tarts   33

K
Kebabs   26-27
Knickerbocker Glory   45

L
Lamb, Barbecued Riblets   13
Lamb Kebabs   26
Lemon Curd Tarts   33
Lime-Lemon Shake   38

M
Macaroni Cheese   30
Milkshakes   38-39

N
Neapolitan Sail Boats   44
No-Bake Cake   41

O
Onion Soup, French   11

P
Pasta-Banger Specials   28
Pastry, Shortcrust   32
Pizzas   18-19
Pork and Bean Hotpot   22
Potatoes, Baked   23
Potato Soup, Quick   10

Q
Quick Cup Cake   42
Quick Potato Soup   10

R
Rosy Salad   17

S
Salad, Rosy   17
Salad, Toadstool   16
Sandwiches   14-15
Sausage Bean Feast   29
Sausage Burgers   25
Scones   35-36
Scrambled Eggs   8
Shortbreads   37
Shortcrust Pastry   32
Soup, French Onion   11
Soup, Quick Potato   10
Spaghetti Bolognese   31
Spaghetti, Speedy Tuna   31
Special Vegetable Layer   21
Spicy Scones   36
Spring Salad Danwich   15
Strawberry Ice Cream Shortbreads   44

T
Toadstool Salad   16
Tuna, Speedy Spaghetti   31

V
Vegetable Kebabs   27
Vegetable Layer   21

W
Wholemeal Scones   36
Winter Pork and Bean Hotpot   22

Y
Yogurt Mallow   45